SCOTLAND
FILM LOCATIONS

Scotland on Screen

Discover the magical settings behind your favourite films and TV shows

A land of mountains and waterfalls, with hundreds of dramatic castles and more than six thousand miles of coast: no wonder so many movie directors head for Scotland. From small-town comedies like *Gregory's Girl* to the epic battles of *Braveheart*, cult classics like *Trainspotting* to Bollywood blockbusters like *Kuch Kuch Hota Hai*, and the global franchises Harry Potter and James Bond, the varied Scottish scenery has provided backdrops for hundreds of films.

A huge number of TV shows have also used Scotland as a setting: *Outlander, The Crown, Shetland, Taggart, Balamory* and *Monarch of the Glen* to name a few of the most successful.

This guidebook tells you where the most popular films and TV serials were made. Walk through Scotland's stunning cities; take the train past lochs and wooded hills, and explore the wild Highlands and Islands to find the most memorably cinematic landscapes.

LEFT Castle DunBroch in the Disney/Pixar film *Brave* was inspired by Dunnottar Castle.

BELOW Scotland has more than 30,000 freshwater lochs.

Harry Potter's Scotland

Spectacular Scottish landscapes bring to life
J.K. Rowling's wizarding world

'I never realized how beautiful this place was,' Harry says to Hermione as they
stand at the window of a Hogwarts tower, overlooking a hill-ringed loch in *Harry
Potter and the Half-Blood Prince* (2009). Hogwarts School of Witchcraft and
Wizardry may be fictional, but the landscape they are looking at is real enough.
Loch Shiel in **Glenfinnan** (p.22) stands in for the Black Lake outside Hogwarts,
location for the Triwizard Tournament's watery second challenge in *Harry Potter
and the Goblet of Fire* (2005).

Glenfinnan is one of twenty-five stops on the **West Highland Line** (p.20) from
Glasgow to Mallaig, Britain's most beautiful railway journey. The iconic image
in the Harry Potter films of the Hogwarts Express steam train puffing over the
Glenfinnan viaduct is a sight you can enjoy in real life – from a train or from
the hills nearby. You can see other Harry Potter locations too from the West
Highland Railway, such as lonely Rannoch Moor where Death Eaters attack
the train, or the wooded island in Loch Eilt where Dumbledore is buried.

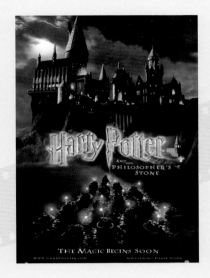

ABOVE Film poster for the UK release of *Harry Potter and the Philosopher's Stone*.

LEFT A wooded island in Loch Eilt was the location for Dumbledore's tomb in the last Harry Potter films.

BELOW The Jacobite steam train puffs along the epic West Highland Railway.

The Clachaig Inn near **Glencoe Village** (p.24) looks out over the rough hillside where Hagrid's hut was built for *Harry Potter and the Prisoner of Azkaban* (2003). Harry's first quidditch match took place in **Glen Nevis** (p.25), an atmospheric valley near the town of Fort William, in the shadow of Britain's highest mountain. Those early views of chimerical Hogwarts School had it perched on the slopes of Ben Nevis, although the actual building used was Alnwick Castle in Northumberland.

Scotland has another important link to Harry Potter besides dramatic film locations. J.K. Rowling did much of her early writing in **Edinburgh** cafés and hotel rooms (p.8). Visitors can see the places where the famous fictional boy wizard was born and the inspirational cityscapes around them. A plaque near the Spoon café on Nicolson Street tells passers by that this is where Rowling wrote some of the early chapters of Harry Potter. The nearby Elephant House also prides itself on being 'the birthplace of Harry Potter' and the iconic Balmoral Hotel is where Rowling finished the last book in the series. The hotel rooms that she stayed in are now the J.K. Rowling suite, furnished with suitably Potteresque touches: a purple door, forest wallpaper and owl statues.

James Bond in Scotland

The Scottish lochs and mountains are 00-heaven for films featuring the Highlands-born spy

Bond's trademark silver Aston Martin is parked in a gloomy, mountainous landscape. Dark figures with guns are reflected in the gleaming, domed wing mirrors. A shoot-out ensues and when the villainous Silva's henchmen are lying dead, Kincade (Albert Finney), gamekeeper of Skyfall Lodge says laconically: 'Welcome to Scotland'. Skyfall Lodge (actually a specially built film set in Surrey) is Bond's fictional ancestral home near **Glen Coe** (p.24) in the Scottish Highlands. His parents lived there and in *Skyfall* (2012) James Bond (Daniel Craig), who has not been back since his parents died when he was a child, returns to his Scottish roots for a dramatic final confrontation.

Edinburgh-born actor Sean Connery was so persuasive as the first cinematic 007 in *Dr. No* (1962) that author Ian Fleming included references to Bond's Scottish heritage when he wrote *You Only Live Twice*, published in 1964. Fleming has M write an obituary when Bond is missing, presumed dead, after a mission

ABOVE Film poster for *Skyfall*, where James Bond returns to his Scottish roots for a dramatic confrontation.

LEFT James Bond (Daniel Craig) stands in front of his famous Aston Martin on the misty road near Glencoe.

BELOW The scenic road through the mountains near Glencoe has starred in numerous movies.

(in the film his death is deliberately faked). We learn that the spy's father, Andrew Bond, came from the village of Glencoe and that, after trouble at Eton, James had transferred to his father's old school, Fettes in **Edinburgh**, where 'the atmosphere was somewhat Calvinistic, and both academic and athletic standards were rigorous'. Fettes College is a real school, near Inverleith Park, and even had – coincidentally – a former pupil called James Bond!

The helicopter-chase scene in *From Russia with Love* (1963) is supposedly somewhere in what is now Croatia. But the rugged green hills that Bond (Sean Connery) hides in to shoot down his pursuers are actually in Scotland. **Loch Craignish**, on the West Coast, provided waters that were calmer than the Adriatic Sea for filming the nail-biting final boat chase.

In *The Spy Who Loved Me* (1977), Bond (now Roger Moore) is briefed about a missing submarine at HM Naval Base Clyde near Faslane, the Royal Navy's Scottish HQ and the UK's nuclear submarine base. **Eilean Donan Castle** (p.28), one of Scotland's most photogenic landmarks, becomes MI6's Scottish HQ in *The World is not Enough* (1999). The mechanical genius Q (at the time still Desmond Llewellyn) shows Bond (Pierce Brosnan) his latest gadgets, including a bagpipe-machine-gun-flamethrower. The same castle appears in the *Highlander* films, in which Sean Connery plays Ramirez, the Immortal.

Blockbusting Edinburgh

Visit Scotland's capital: a cinematic city and the birthplace of Harry Potter

Dozens of films and TV serials have used Edinburgh's distinctive cityscapes as a backdrop: from Walt Disney's version of the city's legend about a loyal dog *Greyfriars Bobby* (1961), to an action-packed sequence in Marvel's 2018 blockbuster, *Avengers: Infinity War*. Avengers Wanda and Vision are walking at night past a café on Edinburgh's Cockburn Street (with a window sign saying 'We will deep fry your kebab'), when Midnight and Glaive ambush them. There's a huge fireball-heavy fight on the Royal Mile and more avengers crash in through the glass roof of Waverley Station. You can ride the lift from the station's platform level up to Market Street for similar views.

Edinburgh is also the birthplace of the huge **Harry Potter** franchise. Loved around the world, the eight films based on J.K. Rowling's novels started life in small cafés in Edinburgh. 'J.K. Rowling wrote some of the early chapters of HARRY POTTER in the rooms on the First Floor of this building', announces a plaque outside **Spoon café**, on the corner of Drummond Street and Nicolson Street. Five minutes away, on George IV Bridge, the cheerful **Elephant House café** also has a plaque outside: 'Made famous as the place of

OPPOSITE The iconic view of Edinburgh from Calton Hill features several much-filmed landmarks.

LEFT In *Greyfriars Bobby* (1961), a Scottish shepherd and his terrier go to Edinburgh.

inspiration to writers such as J.K. Rowling, who sat writing much of her early novels in the back room overlooking Edinburgh Castle.' As well as the castle, the back room also overlooks the churchyard of Greyfriars and – beyond it – the gothic Hogwartian silhouette of George Heriot's School. Edinburgh's architecture was surely influential on Rowling's imaginary world.

Greyfriars Kirkyard is most famous for the 19th-century Skye Terrier who spent 14 years guarding the grave of his master. A statue of the dog stands near the gates and Disney's 1961 film was based on the story of *Greyfriars Bobby*. In *The Prime of Miss Jean Brodie* (1969), Brodie (Maggie Smith, later famous as Professor McGonagall) leads her pupils through the yard from nearby Grassmarket, telling them: 'Observe, little girls, the castle!'

The **National Museum of Scotland** is a must-see for film lovers. Turn right through the Grand Gallery into Kingdom of the Scots to see the Lewis chessmen, which inspired the designers for *Harry Potter and the Philosopher's Stone* (2001). In one of the tense final scenes, Harry, Ron and Hermione engage with dangerous life-size chess pieces. Fans of *Brave* (2012) should also check out the Early

People gallery in the basement; researchers for the movie drew inspiration from the ancient artefacts here, including a huge, battered cauldron. Up on Level 6, you'll find Bonnie Prince Charlie's silver travelling canteen or picnic set (replicated for *Outlander's* Season 2) and a signed poster and script from *Trainspotting* (1996). And don't miss the views from the rooftop garden!

BELOW Danny Boyle's *Trainspotting*, starring Ewan McGregor, Robert Carlyle and Kelly Macdonald, became a cult classic.

Voldemort's tomb? Greyfriars Kirkyard has accidentally become a place of pilgrimage for Potter fans. Several graves, including that of poet William McGonagall, have the classic Scottish names Rowling chose for key characters. In particular, Thomas Riddell, who died in Trinidad in 1802, is buried in the corner nearest Rowling's window. Determined Potterites have been seeking out this tombstone, convinced it has some connection with Tom Riddle aka Lord Voldemort.

Princes Street to Arthur's Seat

With grand shops and hotels against a backdrop of wild mountainsides, the city is packed with film-ready locations

The Victorian **Balmoral Hotel** at one end of Edinburgh's main shopping street has been a city landmark since 1895. In 2007, J.K. Rowling stayed in room 552 while she finished writing the Harry Potter series. The room now has a purple door with a brass owl knocker in her honour and you can just see Rowling's signature on the back of the marble bust of Hermes in the corner turret. Ask at reception to have a look; fans with a very healthy Gringotts account could even spend a night there!

The Balmoral clock tower and the neo-gothic **Scott Monument** are recognisable landmarks on Princes Street that recur in several films like *Cloud Atlas* (2012). Robert Frobisher (Ben Whishaw) climbs the monument, spying on Rufus Sixsmith (James D'Arcy) and says he 'didn't think the view could be any more perfect'.

There's a rousing rendition of 'I Would Walk Five Hundred Miles' on **The Mound**, off Princes Street, at the end of *Sunshine on Leith* (2013), the feel-good musical with Proclaimers' songs. This and other films, like Bollywood comedy *Yeh Hai Jalwa* (2002), feature views and iconic landmarks from nearby **Calton Hill**.

Princes Street's most memorable film appearance is at the start of Danny Boyle's *Trainspotting* (1996). Renton (Ewan McGregor) and Spud (Ewen Bremner) race along Edinburgh's central shopping street with a soundtrack of Iggy Pop's 'Lust for Life' and Renton's famous lines: 'Choose Life, choose a job, choose a career, choose a family...' They leap down the steps onto Calton Road, where Renton is nearly run over. The sequel *T2 Trainspotting* (2017) also has lots of recognisable Edinburgh locations: Renton and Spud go for a sunset run up **Arthur's Seat** with its breathtaking, panoramic views.

Chariots of Fire (1981) has several scenes set in Edinburgh, including one where Arthur's Seat, bathed in golden light, provides the backdrop to an intense conversation between Eric Liddell (Ian Charleson) and his sister Jennie (Cheryl Campbell). Visitors can see a painting of the real Liddell in the Scottish National Portrait Gallery in Queen Street.

One Day (2011) starts with a pre-dawn silhouette of Arthur's Seat, then Calton Hill, Waverley Bridge and the Balmoral Hotel's illuminated clock tower. The film returns to Edinburgh at the end with a flashback: Emma (Anne Hathaway) and Dexter (Jim Sturgess) are climbing **Salisbury Crags**. They look out across the city as he proposes to her and then they race down the slope. Look carefully and you'll see that, on the way, they pass the older Dexter and his daughter, walking up through the same sun-bleached grass.

OPPOSITE Edinburgh's Princes Street, which features at the start of *Trainspotting*.

BELOW LEFT Film poster for *Cloud Atlas*, starring Tom Hanks, Ben Whishaw and Halle Berry.

BELOW *One Day* begins with the young Emma (Anne Hathaway) and Dexter (Jim Sturgess) graduating from Edinburgh University.

Rosslyn Chapel to Tantallon Castle

Da Vinci Code mysteries, tragic Mary Queen of Scots and more in the city suburbs, coast and countryside

The film version of Dan Brown's novel, *The Da Vinci Code* (2006) transformed the fortunes of an atmospheric chapel on a hillside overlooking Roslin Glen. The book sold more than 80 million copies and visitor numbers rocketed, bringing income for much-needed repairs; staff refer to it as 'the Rosslyn miracle'. The **Rosslyn Chapel** is a crucial location in the quest that challenges Robert Langdon (Tom Hanks) and Sophie Neveu (Audrey Tautou).

One clue in *The Da Vinci Code* reads:

The Holy Grail 'neath ancient Roslin waits.
The blade and chalice guarding o'er Her gates.
Adorned in masters' loving art, She lies.
She rests at last beneath the starry skies.

Fifteenth-century Rosslyn (or Roslin) is indeed 'adorned' with a multitude of incredible, medieval stone carvings, which are definitely worth seeing even if you're not a Dan Brown fan. Several interior scenes were filmed in the chapel's basement, but the film's distant view of the chapel used a model because the building was under scaffolding at the time.

The film's penultimate scene, where Robert (Tom Hanks) wonders whether 'maybe human is divine', takes place at nearby **Roslin Castle**; don't miss the easy, ten-minute walk to this atmospheric castle (turn left at the sign beyond the chapel) with views over lovely **Roslin Glen**. Outdoor scenes for the TV series *Outlander* were also filmed in this valley.

On the southern outskirts of Edinburgh, **Craigmillar Castle**, once home to Mary, Queen of Scots, is another atmospheric location – used in *Outlander* as Ardsmuir Prison, where Highlander, Jamie Fraser, is locked up and meets John Grey. The Netflix film, *Outlaw King* (2018), built an elaborate medieval village in front of its forbidding walls for its role as the castle of Robert the Bruce (Chris Pine). Inside, a labyrinth of halls and corridors leads to the battlements and great views over the city.

Outlaw King's Scottish director David Mackenzie has filmed several movies around Edinburgh, including *Young Adam* (2003) and *Hallam Foe* (2007). Look out for **Seacliff Beach**, an hour's drive east of Edinburgh, towards the end of *Outlaw King*. The same beach also appears in the new film of *Mary Queen of Scots* (2018) as Mary (Saoirse Ronan) stares out to sea and says: 'England does not look so different from Scotland.' Ironically, this bit of coast does not look south towards England but north towards Fife. **Tantallon Castle** is visible on the cliffs nearby and its lonely ruins have also

made it into several films, including the unsettling alien movie *Under the Skin* (2013), starring Scarlett Johansson, and the 1998 Bollywood blockbuster, *Kuch Kuch Hota Hai*.

Heading back into Edinburgh, don't miss frequently filmed **Gosford House**. Buy a £1 permit from the farm shop café to walk in the grounds there. The house plays a key role in *Outlander*'s second season and Jackson Brodie (Jason Isaacs, aka Lucius Malfoy) has a fight there in the TV series *Case Histories*, which is filmed all round Edinburgh. Gosford also features in *House of Mirth* (2000), where Lily Bart (Gillian Anderson) meets Lawrence Selden (Eric Stoltz) and they have intense conversations under its ancient trees.

OPPOSITE The 15th-century Rosslyn Chapel is full of incredible, medieval stone carvings.

BELOW *The Da Vinci Code* stars Audrey Tautou as Sophie Neveu and Paul Bettany as Silas.

Leith to Linlithgow

Dockside reunions in *Sunshine on Leith* and loch-side coronations for *Outlaw King*

At the start of *Sunshine on Leith* (2013) two soldiers, happy to be back in their home town, sing 'I'm On My Way' through the Edinburgh streets and arrive beside sunny **Leith Docks**, where they visit the Port O' Leith pub on Constitution Street. Kevin Guthrie (*Fantastic Beasts*) is Ally, who embraces girlfriend Liz on the waterfront. This area of Edinburgh has become a mecca for foodies, with two Michelin-starred restaurants and a lot of great cafés. A slightly grittier side of Leith is on view in *T2 Trainspotting* (2017), which also

features the famous bridges across the Firth of Forth, half an hour's drive to the west. Renton and Sick Boy are taken over the **Forth Road Bridge** in *T2*, dumped naked in the countryside and left to walk back.

Further west still is the lovely town of Linlithgow which has recently become a favourite film location. *Outlaw King* (2018) uses the picturesque exterior of **Linlithgow Palace**, overlooking Linlithgow Loch, as an appropriately majestic setting for the 14th-century coronation of Scottish king Robert the

Bruce. The grassy slope behind the palace becomes a natural amphitheatre with a flotilla of glowing boats sailing across the loch below. The following scene, which shows English horses mustering, was actually filmed in the palace courtyard with its distinctively ornate fountain, while the neighbouring church became a location too.

A few scenes later, things are going less well and the captured Scottish queen, Elizabeth de Burgh (Florence Pugh), is suspended in a cage from the battlements of **Blackness Castle**. This atmospheric waterside fortress, five miles from Linlithgow, also appeared in Franco Zefferelli's 1990 *Hamlet* starring Mel Gibson and Glenn Close and in medieval scenes for the 2008 sci-fi movie *Doomsday*. Most recently, the craggy courtyard at Blackness featured in *Mary Queen of Scots* (2018), starring a flame-haired Saoirse Ronan as Mary and Margot Robbie as Elizabeth I of England.

Outlander is also filmed at Blackness Castle and at elegant **Hopetoun House**, where little Midhope Castle, hidden on the Hopetoun estate, became Lallybroch, Jamie Fraser's family home.

The countryside near Linlithgow was the setting for another Netflix film: *Calibre* (2018), a mesmerising movie as bleak as the wintry landscapes. Scenes were shot in wooded Beecraigs Park, a couple of miles south.

SUNSHINE ON LEITH

OPPOSITE Linlithgow Palace and its crown-topped church stand picturesquely above a loch.

LEFT Poster for the musical *Sunshine on Leith*, which shows off some fabulous Edinburgh settings.

BELOW Filming for *Outlaw King* took place on the slopes below Linlithgow Palace.

Glasgow

Moscow, Stockholm or Philadelphia: the city of many faces

Glasgow has often formed a backdrop for big films and even bigger stars, but it's not always playing itself. It stood in for Stockholm in *The Wife* (2017), where Joan Castleman (Glenn Close) is accompanying her Nobel-winning husband Joe (Jonathan Pryce). In *Cloud Atlas* (2012), the hilly, grid-style roads near **George Street** masqueraded as 1970s San Francisco, where journalist Luisa Rey (Halle Berry) is working.

In *World War Z* (2013), Glasgow doubled as Philadelphia, where Gerry Lane (Brad Pitt) encounters a zombie apocalypse. And for *Florence Foster Jenkins* (2016) Glasgow's West End became 1940s New York: tone-deaf Florence (Meryl Streep) is trying to be an opera singer, with the help of actor St Clair Bayfield (Hugh Grant) who is both her husband and manager.

Stately **George Square**, recognisable in *World War Z*, is one of Glasgow's most-filmed areas. BBC drama *The Secret Agent* (2016) recreated 19th-century London in Edinburgh and Glasgow with the Victorian **City Chambers** becoming the Russian embassy that employs Adolf Verloc

(Toby Jones). The chambers have also doubled as the Vatican in *Heavenly Pursuits* (1986) and the Kremlin in *An Englishman Abroad* (1983).

In *Under the Skin* (2013), Scarlett Johansson plays a mysterious alien creature disguised as a human woman. The city she wanders through is Glasgow, seen through new eyes: she stumbles through **Trongate**, drives past Celtic Park football stadium after a (real) match and buys clothes in the busy Buchanan Galleries shopping centre. The city becomes less familiar as viewers are drawn into a strange and disturbing otherworld.

The fairy-lit House of Fraser department store on **Buchanan Street** provides a jollier setting for the Christmassy opening of Bill Forsyth's

comedy, *Comfort and Joy* (1984). Don't miss the Tardis-style police box as you stroll up Buchanan Street. Nearby Mitchell Lane, with the Lighthouse, is a location in Ken Loach's whisky-related comedy, *The Angel's Share* (2012). Glasgow has featured in several of Ken Loach's films, including *My Name is Joe* (1998) and *Sweet Sixteen* (2002).

Kelvingrove Park is another photogenic area, doubling as 1950s Boston in *Outlander* and as 1950s London for *Rillington Place* (2016), the BBC drama about serial killer John Christie. For *House of Mirth* (2000), Kelvingrove Art Gallery became New York's Grand Central Station. Across the River Clyde is gritty Govan, where BBC Scotland's *Rab C Nesbitt* was set.

A city view from the top of Glasgow's Rennie Mackintosh-designed **Lighthouse** sets the scene in STV's *Taggart*, where so often: 'There's been a murder.'

OPPOSITE Glasgow's City Chambers, a popular film location, overlook George Square.

BELOW Brad Pitt's *World War Z* turned Glasgow into apocalyptic Philadelphia.

Around Glasgow

From the medieval cathedral to Cumbernauld shopping centre, varied landscapes around Glasgow have been caught on camera

In *Outlaw King* (2018) Glasgow's medieval cathedral became Greyfriars Kirk, Dumfries, where Robert the Bruce killed John Comyn, his rival for the crown of Scotland. The picturesque neighbouring **Necropolis** featured in *Restless Natives* (1985), Michael Hoffman's cult Scottish comedy.

Fans of *Gregory's Girl* (1980) can make a quirky pilgrimage to the Abronhill area of **Cumbernauld**, north-east of Glasgow. The school and the old red phone box are long gone, but the distinctive apartment blocks and underpasses still feel familiar; the chip shop (Trio on Larch Road) and **Oak Road playing fields** are still there. The iconic giant clock where Gregory (John Gordon Sinclair) waits for Dorothy (Dee Hepburn) is in a disused part of the **Antonine shopping centre.** Ask at the management centre on the first floor and they will take you through the locked doors to see it.

Glasgow as Edinburgh Danny Boyle shot several scenes in Glasgow (pretending to be Edinburgh) in his tense first film for cinema, *Shallow Grave* (1994). He also used a forested location in **Rouken Glen**, south of Glasgow, as the place where flatmates Alex (Ewan McGregor), David (Christopher Eccleston) and Juliet (Kerry Fox) try to bury the dismembered body of the mysterious Hugo (Keith Allen).

Cross the railway from Abronhill to visit **Cumbernauld House Park** where Gregory and Susan (Clare Grogan) have their date at the end of the film. A couple of miles away, Wardpark studios are the home of TV drama *Outlander*. Several woodland scenes for *Outlander* have been filmed in nearby **Cumbernauld Glen**, which doubles as American forests for Season 4.

OPPOSITE Glasgow's imposing cathedral, viewed from the neighbouring Necropolis.

RIGHT Poster for *Shallow Grave*, where three flatmates bury their mysterious lodger in the woods.

LEFT In *Gregory's Girl*, Gregory (John Gordon Sinclair) falls in love with footballer Dorothy (Dee Hepburn).

West Highland Line

Harry Potter, James Bond and the boys from
Trainspotting have all been filmed at locations
along Britain's most beautiful railway

'Now what?' asks Sick Boy, in *Trainspotting* (1996), as a train pulls away from an isolated railway station. 'We go for a walk,' says Tommy, pointing across the trackless wilderness to a mountain with patches of snow still clinging to its sides. 'Doesn't it make you proud to be Scottish?' shouts Tommy, heading for the mountain, as the other three sit down and start drinking and Renton launches into a rant: 'It's shite being

Scottish!' The remote station is **Corrour**, the wild heath is Rannoch Moor, the mountain is called Leum Uilleim, and the railway is the West Highland Line, one of the most scenic train journeys in the world.

Setting off from Glasgow, the train passes the Faslane naval base, where James Bond (Roger Moore) is briefed on the missing submarine in *The Spy Who Loved Me* (1977). It's located near

Garelochhead station, on the shores of a wooded sea loch. The train runs on along the famously 'bonnie banks' of Loch Lomond and splits in two at Crianlarich, with the more-filmed line heading over the moors to Fort William and Mallaig.

The **West Highland Railway** itself is famous on screen as the route of the Hogwarts Express. It starts from Glasgow's Queen Street station and takes three hours to reach **Rannoch Moor**. The Fort William area, another hour beyond Rannoch, has provided locations for several movies, including Mel Gibson's *Braveheart* (1995).

LEFT The West Highland Railway passes through a remote and beautiful landscape.

BELOW The iconic, horseshoe-shaped viaduct at Glenfinnan appears in several Harry Potter movies.

Travel tip A return ticket from Glasgow to Fort William is about £50, but – if you book in advance – you can find tickets online from £10 each way.

Glenfinnan and beyond

Continue Britain's most magical train ride and discover a memorial to Jacobite warriors and Dumbledore's island

There's more spectacular railway beyond **Fort William**. In summer, the popular Jacobite steam train recreates the full Hogwarts Express experience or you can see the same views all year round more cheaply from the standard ScotRail trains. The fifth station is **Glenfinnan**, famous for its huge, curving viaduct. The Hogwarts Express is often filmed crossing it and, in *Chamber of Secrets* (2002), Harry Potter finds himself hanging out of a flying Ford Anglia while Ron drives it above and below the viaduct.

Get off at Glenfinnan for a closer look and to visit the Station Museum on the opposite platform. This friendly heritage centre has a tearoom and bunkhouse in old train carriages, rail memorabilia, information about the viaduct and great local walking maps. The Viaduct Trail is an adventurous circular walk of about three miles, which gives visitors a close-up view of this marvel of engineering, with its twenty-one towering arches.

Nearby, the National Trust's visitor centre has a year-round café, an

exhibition about the Jacobites and tickets to climb the **Glenfinnan Monument** – a memorial to the highlanders who died fighting for Bonnie Prince Charlie in 1745. The view from the monument across Loch Shiel includes more Harry Potter locations, including the 'Black Lake' where the second challenge in the Triwizard Tournament was held in *Goblet of Fire*. To see more of the loch, take a cruise from near the Glenfinnan House Hotel.

Between Glenfinnan and the next station, heading on towards Mallaig, the West Highland Railway runs alongside Loch Eilt. Look out towards the end of the loch for the island covered in Scots pine trees, where Dumbledore is buried in *Harry Potter and the Deathly Hallows*. The white sandy beaches around Morar, the penultimate station, appeared in *Local Hero* (1983, see p.40), *Monarch of the Glen* (2000–2005, p.26) and the end of *Breaking the Waves* (1996).

ABOVE Beyond the Glenfinnan viaduct, Loch Shiel was used as one of the settings for Hogwarts in *Harry Potter and the Goblet of Fire*.

BELOW In *Chamber of Secrets*, Harry Potter finds himself hanging out of a flying Ford Anglia above the Glenfinnan viaduct.

Immortal heroes Christopher Lambert, the hero of the fantasy *Highlander* (1986), tells Brenda: 'I am Connor MacLeod of the Clan MacLeod. I was born in the village of Glenfinnan on the shores of Loch Shiel, and I am immortal.' The loch is where Ramirez (Sean Connery) tips MacLeod into the water from a rowing boat.

Glen Coe and Glen Nevis

James Bond, Harry Potter and other cinematic legends come to life in these quintessential Highland valleys

The mountain pass at **Glen Coe** is so distinctively 'Scottish' it has become almost synonymous with the country's wild countryside. James Bond's Aston Martin DB5 flashes silver on the misty road as he heads back towards his gloomy childhood home in *Skyfall* (2012). James Bond (Daniel Craig) and M (Judi Dench) pause on the road near the rushing **River Etive** before driving on towards the rugged moorland beyond.

Scottish actor Robbie Coltrane plays ex-KGB agent Valentin Dmitrovich Zukovsky in two Bond films and

Rubeus Hagrid in Harry Potter. Hagrid's hut and other crucial locations were built at Glen Coe for *Harry Potter and the Prisoner of Azkaban* (2004). The view from the window of the cosy **Clachaig Inn,** less than a mile from the Glen Coe visitors' centre, is the backdrop for the hut and its pumpkin patch. Hannah (Michelle Monaghan) is staying at the inn in *Made of Honour* (2008) before getting married at Eilean Donan (p.28).

The Highland skies are grey, the hills above **Kinlochleven** are craggy and Rob Roy (Liam Neeson) strides over the grass to where a gang of cattle thieves are resting. The scene, near the start of *Rob Roy* (1995), shot entirely in Scotland, establishes both the main character's authority and the leading role of the film's dramatic Highland scenery.

The nearby waterfall known as the **Meeting of Three Waters** marks another location for film fans: the Bridge of Death and the Gorge of Eternal Peril (with a few added fireworks and smoke machines) in *Monty Python and the Holy Grail* (1975). A twenty-minute drive south, on Loch Linnhe, is picturesque **Castle Stalker** that features at the end of the film as the 'Castle of Aaaaarrrrggggghhhh'. Most of the Pythons' other castle scenes were filmed at Doune Castle (p.34).

Beyond the town of Fort William, in the shadow of Ben Nevis, highest mountain in Britain, is another much-filmed valley. Controversially,

Braveheart (1995) was mostly shot in Ireland, but the village where William Wallace (Mel Gibson) lives at the start of the film was built in the hills beside **Glen Nevis**. The Forestry Commission has a Braveheart car park nearby with the legendary Wishing Stone on the edge of it.

Glen Nevis is also the setting for Harry Potter's first quidditch match in *The Philosopher's Stone* (2001). The distinctive **Steall Falls**, further east along Glen Nevis, appear behind the quidditch arena in *The Half Blood Prince* (2009). To reach the falls, Scotland's second highest waterfall, is a Potteresque adventure: drive to the end of the road beside the River Nevis and walk the last mile. An ominous sign announces: 'Danger of Death' and the path gets rockier as it climbs with streams tumbling over it into the gorge far below.

ABOVE Mel Gibson as William Wallace in *Braveheart*.

OPPOSITE Glen Coe, with its winding road and majestic mountains, represents quintessentially beautiful Scottish scenery.

LEFT Hagrid's hut in *Harry Potter and the Prisoner of Azkaban* was built opposite the Clachaig Inn near Glencoe Village.

Loch Laggan and Loch Ness

From *Monarch of the Glen* to Queen Elizabeth and Queen Victoria, the Highlands are a royal retreat

'How can you own a view?' Katrina asks the reluctant new Laird of Glenbogle, Archie MacDonald, (Alastair Mackenzie) in the popular TV series, *Monarch of the Glen* (2000–2005). They are talking on the edge of Loch Laggan, with the woods and hills behind them and he confesses that he misses 'the water, the hills', but doesn't want 'to live in a freezing castle'. The 'castle', turreted Glenbogle House, was really **Ardverikie**, on the shores of

Loch Laggan, a forty-five-minute drive from Fort William. It is into the waters of this loch, boasting Britain's largest freshwater beach, that Hector MacDonald (Richard Briers) falls off his jet ski near the start of episode one.

The Ardverikie estate also appears in the popular Netflix drama, *The Crown*, where it stands in for Balmoral in the first two series. Queen Elizabeth

DAME JUDI DENCH   BILLY CONNOLLY

HER MAJESTY

Mrs. BROWN

"Gutsy and Compelling!★★★★"
– Empire

ABOVE Film Poster for *Mrs. Brown*, which sees Queen Victoria (Judi Dench) and John Brown (Billy Connolly) develop an unexpected friendship.

LEFT The view of Ardverikie House across Loch Laggan, as seen in *Monarch of the Glen*.

The remote landscapes under the aeroplane in the tense opening scene of *The Dark Knight Rises* (2012) were filmed around Loch Glass, about an hour's drive north of Loch Ness.

Enjoy your own boat trip on legendary Loch Ness under the beautifully ruined walls of **Urquhart Castle**, twenty miles north. In the movie *Loch Ness* (1996), John Dempsey (Ted Danson) is sent to Scotland to investigate the mythical monster and stays at a hotel run by Laura McFetridge (Joely Richardson). There are some establishing shots of Loch Ness, but the village scenes were shot on the west coast. There's a view of Urquhart Castle in *The Water Horse* (2007) as the monster swims along the loch.

BELOW The baronial-style turrets of Ardverikie have doubled as Balmoral in *The Crown*.

(Clare Foy) has a picnic with her mother in the wooded grounds beside a picturesque stream. And the numerous streams and loch side are the idyllic setting for the Scottish sections of *Salmon Fishing in the Yemen* (2011), where Ardverikie plays the sheikh's house in Scotland.

There are more royal visits in *Mrs. Brown* (1997) when Queen Victoria (Judi Dench) and John Brown (Billy Connolly) develop their unorthodox friendship. Queen Victoria really did stay here in the summer of 1847 and the queen's barge sailed on Loch Laggan. Although the estate is only open to people booking weddings there or staying in one of the self-catering cottages, there are views of the castle's baronial-style turrets from the opposite shore of the loch.

Eilean Donan

Follow in the footsteps of Hollywood and Bollywood A-listers, from Errol Flynn to Pierce Brosnan and Shah Rukh Khan

In the cult classic *Highlander* (1986), **Eilean Donan** is the castle of Clan MacLeod, which, until he is exiled, is home to the Immortal Connor MacLeod. Ramirez (Sean Connery) tutors him in the surrounding Highlands. Revealed in flashbacks from MacLeod's life in 1980s New York, Eilean Donan is busy with tartan-wearing warriors and cross-bearing monks. Visitors will find this 13th-century restored castle looking camera-ready, perched on its small rocky island, backed by wooded hills, and joined to the mainland by an arched bridge with mist sometimes rising from the waters around it.

The castle has also featured in *Loch Ness* (1996), where it stood in for Castle Urquhart as a backdrop for sightings of the famous monster, and, earlier, in *Bonnie Prince Charlie* (1948), with David Niven as the Jacobite prince. The same backdrop is used in *The Master of Ballantrae* (1953), where Jamie Durie (Errol Flynn) returns to the ancestral Durrisdeer estate. He appears to swing on the chandelier in Eilean Donan's hall and escape via a fireplace.

Several movies, including Bollywood blockbuster *Kuch Kuch Hota Hai* (1998) have filmed the outside of the castle. Some films seem to venture inside, but the interiors are usually studio reconstructions. Inside the real castle are narrow spiral staircases, stone-flagged floors and tartan-draped four posters with great views from tiny wood-framed windows. The lively kitchen, with rabbits hanging in the larder and jars of pickles on the shelves, feels like a film set.

In *The World Is Not Enough* (1999), we first see a classic exterior view with added aerials and satellite dishes and the caption 'MI6 Headquarters Scotland' as MI6 chief of staff Bill Tanner (Michael Kitchen, best known from the TV series *Foyle's War*) explains a fiendish plot involving exploding money. The briefing appears to take place in a wood-panelled version of the castle's banqueting hall.

The World is not Enough has several Scottish connections: as well as Q (Desmond Llewelyn's final performance in the role) showing Bond some lethal bagpipes, Glasgow-born Robert Carlyle (*Trainspotting, The Full Monty*) plays Renard, the vengeful terrorist with a bullet in his brain, and Edinburgh-born Shirley Manson sings the soulful theme song. Robert Carlyle also spent years filming in the Highlands as the eponymous police constable in *Hamish Macbeth* (1995–1997). The village of Plockton became the small town of Lochdubh where Hamish Macbeth is a constable.

OPPOSITE A dramatic sky above floodlit Eilean Donan, one of Scotland's most photographed castles.

BELOW Christopher Lambert played the Highlander Connor MacLeod, one of a race of immortal warriors who can only die when they are beheaded.

Skye

The island's enchanting beauty is perfect for fantasy and science fiction, from *Stardust* to *Flash Gordon*

Connected to the Scottish mainland by a road bridge and ferries, Skye is fifty miles long and the largest island of the Inner Hebrides. Almost every corner has attracted film makers, from the lighthouse at **Neist Point** on the far western tip in *Breaking the Waves* (1996) to the Kylerhea ferry in *Made of Honour* (2008).

Several legends associated with the Isle of Skye involve giants so it seems appropriate that the visual team behind Steven Spielberg's *The BFG* (2016), who previously worked on the *Lord of the Rings* films, have turned the

island's geography, from the Quiraing landslip to the volcanic **Cullin Mountains**, into the fictional Giant Country. The softly-spoken Big Friendly Giant (Mark Rylance) takes little Sophie to this land of giants when she sees him through the window of her London orphanage. *The BFG* also features the grassy hills of Skye's **Fairy Glen**, where Ditchwater Sal parks her caravan in *Stardust* – suitably magical settings for these supernatural stories.

The island's epic rock formations were one of many global locations for

Transformers: The Last Knight (2017). And in *Flash Gordon* (1980) Flash got on a small plane, which Ming the Merciless (Max von Sydow) hits with a meteorite, at Broadford, the island's aerodrome. Robbie Coltrane (later famous as Hagrid) acted in his first film role there as an airfield worker.

The jagged hills of the **Quiraing** in northern Skye can be seen behind Macbeth (Michael Fassbender), in the gruesome and powerful 2015 film, as he rides home from battle and is made Thane of Cawdor. You see them again later behind Lady Macbeth (Marion Cotillard). Lady Macduff (Elizabeth Debicki, who played Jed in *The Night Manager*) is murdered in the picturesque Sligachan Glen some way south.

The distinctive Quiraing also lends its power to the witch Lamia (Michelle Pfeiffer) in *Stardust*. The beautiful, evil Queen Ravenna (Charlize Theron) orders the huntsman (Chris Hemsworth) to cross it in pursuit of Snow White (Kristen Stewart) in *Snow White and the Huntsman* (2012).

The unmistakable pointy rock known as the **Old Man of Storr** is a favourite when creating enchanted landscapes. Near the start of Ridley Scott's star-studded sci-fi film, *Prometheus* (2012), two archaeologists find a star map in a cave underneath the Old Man. Stopping nearby for refreshments in colourful **Portree**, Skye's largest town, you might remember that there's a quidditch team in *Harry Potter and the Order of the Phoenix* called the Pride of Portree.

Originally released as a B movie, *The Wicker Man* (1973) has developed a cult following. The action starts in the town of **Plockton**, on the mainland, and the opening images show a seaplane flying over the island, passing the Old Man of Storr. Later scenes were filmed around Culzean Castle, fifty miles south of Glasgow.

OPPOSITE **The distinctive landscape of Skye is a popular cinematic backdrop, for instance in** *Macbeth* (2015) **starring Michael Fassbender.**

BELOW *The Wicker Man*, **a disturbing 1970s classic, starts in Plockton near Skye.**

From the writer of 'Frenzy & Sleuth' Anthony Shaffer's incredible occult thriller

THE WICKER MAN

Starring
Edward Woodward
Britt Ekland
Diane Cilento
Ingrid Pitt
And
Christopher Lee
as Lord Summerisle

Produced by Peter Snell
Directed by Robin Hardy
Screenplay by Anthony Shaffer

LEFT **The Quiraing features in** *The BFG*, **when the Big Friendly Giant (Mark Rylance) takes little Sophie to the land of giants.**

Inner and Outer Hebrides

Children's shows, comedies, crime series and more have been filmed among the varied Scottish islands

There are nearly 800 islands off the coast of Scotland. From long, sandy beaches to craggy, cloud-topped mountains, ancient stone circles to brightly painted seafronts, film makers have plenty of scenes to choose from.

'Can you see all the different coloured houses sitting by the sea?' starts the song in the much-loved BBC show *Balamory* (2002–2005). This cheerful educational series focussed on an invented island community, but the colourful row of houses that faces the bay in **Tobermory** on the island of

Mull are real. They are mostly private houses, but Mull, with its beaches and boat trips, walks and wildlife, is a great place for a family holiday. Edie McCredie's (blue) house is now the Tobermory Chocolate factory and Josie Jump's (yellow) house is the Park Lodge Hotel.

Mull was also a major location for the classic romance, *I Know Where I'm Going* (1945). Joan Webster (Wendy Hiller) knows she's going to the Hebrides to get married, but bad weather strands her on Mull, where

For Balamory fans that can't make it to Mull, the big pink house, which belonged to Archie (Miles Jupp), is Fenton Tower, a rentable castle half an hour's drive from Edinburgh, and Edie McCredie's bus is in the (brilliant) Glasgow Museum of Transport.

she gets to know the locals. She visits doomed, atmospheric Moy Castle and gets caught in the Corryvreckan whirlpool.

There's something unearthly about the landscapes of the Scottish islands. Stanley Kubrick clearly thought so when he chose the Outer Hebrides as a location for *2001: A Space Odyssey* (1968). The strange planet that astronaut David Bowman sees below him near the end of the film is the island of **Harris**.

The **Calanais Stones** (or Callanish) are one of many stone circles on the island of Lewis in the Outer Hebrides. Made nearly five millennia ago and used for Bronze age rituals, they have a powerful aura about them even today. The Pixar animation *Brave* (2012), set in medieval Scotland, has several scenes featuring a mysterious stone circle that is clearly based on Calanais. They also influenced the designers

working on the TV show *Outlander*, for which the (polystyrene) circle was relocated to a wooded hill near Rannoch Moor.

The village of Castlebay on the island of **Barra**, to the south, was the location for the Ealing Comedy *Whisky Galore!* (1949). A freighter carrying 50,000 cases of whisky is shipwrecked off the fictional island of Todday, where the wartime supply of whisky has run out. The story is based on real events, when the SS *Politician* sank off Eriskay in 1941. A 2016 remake was filmed in Aberdeenshire, with Eddie Izzard as Captain Waggett.

A hundred miles from the Scottish mainland, the most northerly part of the British Isles, the **Shetland Islands** are a unique archipelago. The TV crime series *Shetland* is set and partly filmed there. Season 5 is expected in 2019 with Douglas Henshall still starring as DI Jimmy Perez.

OPPOSITE The colourful row of seafront houses in Tobermory on the Isle of Mull were fictionalised in the children's show *Balamory*.

BELOW The animation *Brave*, set in a mythical medieval Scotland, features a mysterious stone circle based on Calanais on Lewis in the Outer Hebrides.

Doune Castle

Game of Thrones, Monty Python and *Outlander*
have put this 14th-century fort on the map

Medieval **Doune Castle**, towering over the River Teith near Stirling, has been a star of the screen since *Monty Python and the Holy Grail* (1975). The Monty Python team used different shots of Doune to give the impression of several different castles. The film opens with the sound of horses in the mist as King Arthur (Graham Chapman) trots towards the castle on foot with his servant Patsy (Terry Gilliam) banging coconut shells together to sound like hooves. Standing under the east wall, he introduces himself as 'King of the

Britons…' ('Pull the other one,' says a voice from the castle).

Various rooms inside Doune Castle were used to film the most memorable scenes in *Holy Grail*: the 'Camelot' song (Great Hall), Castle Anthrax (the kitchens), Swamp Castle (Duchess's Hall), the wedding scene (the courtyard) and more. Monty Python fans have been visiting Doune for years to trot round the walls with coconut shells, shouting lines like 'I fart in your general direction' (in cod French accents). The only other

Scottish castle in the film is Castle Stalker (p.25).

Monty Python's actor/director Terry Jones narrates Doune's audio guide, complete with comic sound effects, explaining: 'in 1974 some friends and myself made a very silly film…' The guide has optional extras for fans, like the fact that the wooden Trojan Rabbit was winched up from a van hidden inside the gate, along with audio clips from the film ('Boinnnggg… Run away! Run away!')

Doune was used in a pilot episode of *Game of Thrones* for exterior shots of Winterfell. Later *Game of Thrones* filming moved to Northern Ireland, but the Scottish castle struck cinematic gold again when Doune became Castle Leoch, fictional seat of the Clan Mackenzie, in *Outlander*. Sam Hueghan (who plays Jamie Fraser) has

added further sections to Doune's entertaining audio guide.

Most recently, Doune Castle featured towards the end of *Outlaw King* (2018), the Netflix Robert Bruce biopic, as Douglas Castle. It is one of several castles Bruce and his men burn rather than leave for the English. Nicki Scott, cultural resources advisor for Historic Environment Scotland, praised the skill of the film's art department and admitted: 'it was rather unsettling seeing Doune Castle "on fire", even knowing it was special effects!'

OPPOSITE The sturdy ruins of medieval Doune Castle have become a popular star of the screen.

BELOW *Monty Python and the Holy Grail* uses different sides of Doune to represent various fantastical castles.

Drummond Castle Gardens

Visit the 'Scottish Versailles' with its regal formality, or the nearby glens and beaches from *Chariots of Fire*

As a backdrop to Tim Roth's camply villainous aristocrat in *Rob Roy* (1995), **Drummond Castle**'s formal gardens make a striking contrast to the wild Highlands in the earlier scenes. Dastardly estate manager Killearn (Brian Cox) can be seen striding through the stone archway into Drummond's courtyard with tartan-wearing Rob Roy. They turn right through the wrought iron gates onto the top terrace and a classic view of

the gardens is spread out in front of them.

You can visit these gardens from April to October; its box hedges form a giant saltire cross like a Scottish flag, but are picked out in floral red and yellow rather than white and blue. In *Rob Roy*, Drummond Castle is the on-screen home of the Marquis of Montrose (John Hurt), who has his portrait painted among the topiary and statues. Drummond's other film appearances include *Man to Man* (2005), in which Kristin Scott-Thomas and Joseph Fiennes play Victorian anthropologists.

In the TV show *Outlander's* second season, Drummond gardens double as Versailles for an electrifying rendezvous with an old enemy. In this idyllic summer setting, with roses in full flower and flamboyant courtly French costumes, Claire Fraser (Catriona Balfe) encounters evil Jack Randall (Tobias Menzies) and unwillingly presents him to King Louis (Lionel Lingleser, who also plays

Léopold in Netflix 2019 sci-fi drama, *Osmosis*).

The **Abercairny Estate** nearby, was the setting for the (digitally created) River Run mansion in *Outlander's* Season 4. Five miles north, the athletics meeting in *Chariots of Fire* (1981), promoted as 'Highlands of Scotland 1926', actually took place in a valley known as the **Sma' Glen**. Still further north, Queen Victoria visited **Blair Castle** several times and ITV's *Victoria* filmed there, when the on-screen queen (Jenna Coleman of *Doctor Who* fame) rode one of the estate's horses.

OPPOSITE The geometric design of Drummond Castle gardens looks like a giant Scottish flag; in autumn the gardens are especially beautiful.

BELOW The opening of *Chariots of Fire*, where the white-clad athletes race barefoot through the surf, was filmed on the beach at St Andrews.

Chariots of Fire's most memorable location is an hour's drive east of Perth in the coastal town of St Andrews. The beach that the athletes run along at the start of the film is **West Sands**. The sight of it makes many movie lovers want to race through the surf while singing Vangelis's stirring theme music at the tops of their voices.

Dunnottar Castle

One of Scotland's most dramatic castles has set the scene for *Hamlet* and *Brave*

Towers and battlements perch on a ring of cliffs above the water; it's clear that when the animators created Merida's castle in the Pixar film *Brave* (2012), they had **Dunnottar Castle** near Aberdeen in mind. To see the castle in all its picturesque glory, follow the cliff-top path from the nearby town of Stonehaven.

King Fergus (with the voice of Billy Connolly) and Queen Elinor (Emma Thompson) rule the kingdom of DunBroch, a fantasy landscape full of iconic Scottish images: the castle on its craggy coastal promontory, ruins of an even older fort nearby, a stone circle, a valley where the Highland games take place, an ancient forest and a waterfall cascading down the cliffs. You can find examples of all these around Dunnottar Castle. The designers may have had the Calanais

stone circle in mind (p.33), but Clune Hill, twenty minutes' drive from Stonehaven, has a ring of red granite stones, where you might easily meet a will-o'-the-wisp. **Dunnottar Woods** nearby are ideal for family strolls, with a shell-covered summerhouse and little waterfall-filled bathing place.

Harry Potter star Daniel Radcliffe filmed at Dunnottar when he played Igor, assistant to the famous scientist (Scottish actor James McAvoy), in *Victor Frankenstein* (2015). The castle is often seen in darkness and pouring rain, which is what director Franco Zefferelli was hoping for when he

Fit for a prince If you stay in Stonehaven, don't miss the award-winning fish and chips from The Bay or the irresistible Italian ice creams at Giulianotti's vintage sweetshop.

chose Dunnottar to be brooding Elsinore castle in his film of *Hamlet* (1990). Mel Gibson played the prince, five years before *Braveheart*, and remembers that instead of 'dark and angry weather' it was as sunny as Miami!

ABOVE Sunrise behind the dramatic cliff-top ruins of Dunnottar Castle.

RIGHT Dunnottar became Elsinore castle in Zefferelli's 1990 film of *Hamlet*, starring Mel Gibson.

Around Aberdeen

From *Local Hero* to *The Crown*, Scotland's east coast has its iconic moments

A red phone box ringing by the harbour at night is the memorable last image from *Local Hero* (1983), which won Bill Forsyth a BAFTA for best director. Macintyre, an American oil company executive, is sent to Scotland to buy up a coastal village and turn it into a refinery. Together with local rep Danny Oldsen (a young Peter Capaldi) he moves into Ferness for a few weeks. Ferness is actually **Pennan**, north of Aberdeen, a tiny village with a single row of whitewashed houses facing the harbour. The famous **phone box**, where Macintyre describes the Aurora Borealis to his boss Felix Happer (Burt Lancaster), was originally a prop, removed after filming. Another phone box was later installed by popular demand.

The **sandy beach** is actually on the far side of the country near Mallaig (p.23); the production team built a church by the beach so the two scenes could match up. Forsyth has since admitted that, with a background in realism and documentaries, he wasn't sure at first that this cinematic trickery would work as well as it does. He describes the process of shifting the cast and crew from one coast to the other as 'like a circus moving'.

Netflix drama *The Crown* featured ruined **Slains Castle**, north of Aberdeen, in Season 1. The grieving Queen Mother (Victoria Hamilton) rides her horse along a beach and spots a dilapidated seaside mansion that she does up as a holiday home. The real Castle of Mey, on Scotland's north coast, spotted by the actual queen mum in 1952, is fully restored and open to visitors from May to September. Season 3 of *The Crown* (2019) covers events in the late 1960s and beyond with an older cast that includes Olivia Coleman as Queen Elizabeth and Tobias Menzies (*Outlander*) as Prince Philip.

In Stephen Frears' BAFTA-winning drama *The Queen* (2006), Cluny Castle near Aberdeen stood in for Balmoral, the British royal family's baronial-style Scottish palace. After an establishing glimpse of the real Balmoral, also in Aberdeenshire, the ornate interior is mostly filmed at Cluny, which is not generally open to the public. Visitors can head to nearby Castle Fraser, where Elizabeth (Oscar-winning Helen Mirren) sees the mythical stag. Castle Fraser, which belongs to National Trust for Scotland, is a fairy-tale tower house with a walled garden and tearoom.

OPPOSITE The ruins of Slains Castle appeared in Season 1 of *The Crown*.

BELOW The village of Pennan was a key setting for the feel-good film *Local Hero*.

Places to Visit

www.visitscotland.com

Ardverikie Estate (private)
https://www.ardverikie.com/

Balmoral Hotel
https://www.grandluxuryhotels.com/hotel/
balmoral-hotel

Beecraigs Park
https://www.westlothian.gov.uk/beecraigs

Blackness Castle
https://www.historicenvironment.scot/visit-a-
place/places/blackness-castle/

Calanais Stones
https://www.historicenvironment.scot/visit-a-
place/places/calanais-standing-stones/

Calton Hill
https://ewh.org.uk/world-heritage-sites/
calton-hill/

Castle Fraser
https://www.nts.org.uk/visit/places/castle-
fraser

Cumbernauld House Park
https://www.northlanarkshire.gov.uk/index.
aspx?articleid=6769

Doune Castle
https://www.historicenvironment.scot/visit-a-
place/places/doune-castle/

Drummond Castle Gardens
https://www.drummondcastlegardens.co.uk/

Dunnottar Castle
https://www.dunnottarcastle.co.uk/

Eilean Donan Castle
https://www.eileandonancastle.com/

Elephant House café
http://www.elephanthouse.biz/

Forth Bridges
https://www.theforthbridges.org/

Glasgow City Chambers
https://www.glasgow.gov.uk/index.
aspx?articleid=19136

Glen Coe Visitor Centre NTS
https://www.nts.org.uk/visit/places/glencoe

Glen Nevis Visitor Centre
http://ben-nevis.com/visitor-center/visitor-
center.php

**Glenfinnan station
(and start of viaduct trail)**
https://glenfinnanstationmuseum.co.uk/

**Glenfinnan Monument Visitor Centre
NTS**
https://www.nts.org.uk/visit/places/glenfinnan-
monument

Gosford House
http://www.gosfordhouse.co.uk/

Greyfriars Kirkyard
https://greyfriarskirk.com/visit-us

Hopetoun House
http://hopetoun.co.uk/

House of Fraser, Glasgow
https://www.houseoffraser.co.uk/store/
glasgow/1529

Jacobite steam train
https://www.westcoastrailways.co.uk/jacobite/
jacobite-steam-train-details.cfm

Lighthouse, Glasgow
http://www.thelighthouse.co.uk/

Linlithgow Palace
https://www.historicenvironment.scot/visit-a-
place/places/linlithgow-palace/

Loch Shiel cruises
https://www.highlandcruises.co.uk/

Museum of Transport, Glasgow
https://www.glasgowlife.org.uk/museums/
venues/riverside-museum

National Museum of Scotland
https://www.nms.ac.uk/national-museum-of-
scotland/

Pennan
https://www.undiscoveredscotland.co.uk/
pennan/pennan/index.html

Rosslyn Chapel
https://www.rosslynchapel.com/

Rouken Glen
http://www.roukenglenpark.co.uk/

Scott Monument
https://www.edinburghmuseums.org.uk/venue/
scott-monument

Shetland Islands
https://www.shetland.org/

Slains Castle
https://www.undiscoveredscotland.co.uk/
crudenbay/slainscastle/index.html

Spoon café
https://spoonedinburgh.co.uk/

Tantallon Castle
https://www.historicenvironment.scot/visit-a-
place/places/tantallon-castle/

Tobermory
http://www.tobermory.co.uk/

Urquhart Castle
https://www.historicenvironment.scot/visit-a-
place/places/urquhart-castle/

West Highland Railway
https://www.scotrail.co.uk/scotland-by-rail/
great-scenic-rail-journeys/west-highland-line-
glasgow-oban-and-fort-williammallaig